# YOU CAN PROSPER WITH AI

*Ideas To Create, Work, And Thrive In the AI Age*

ACHIENG ORETA

## TABLE OF CONTENTS

INTRODUCTION……….3

1: WHAT IS AI, HOW IT WORKS AND WHY NOW?..........6

2: NEW RULES FOR THE AI ECONOMY……….12

3: INVESTING IN ARTIFICIAL INTELLIGENCE……….16

4: CONTROLLING YOUR DIGITAL FOOTPRINT……….23

5: BECOMING AI FLUENT……….32

6: NAVIGATING AN AI POWERED WORKPLACE……….37

7: BUILDING A BUSINESS IN THE AI AGE……….43

8: MONETIZATION……….52

9: AUTONOMOUS AI AGENTS……….70

10: CREATIVITY AND ARTS IN THE AI AGE……….73

11: THE FUTURE OF AI……….80

12: SOME AI TOOLS TO SUPPORT YOUR JOURNEY……….86

# INTRODUCTION

Let's be honest. Most of us don't wake up thinking about the Industrial Revolution or the early days of the internet. And really, why would we? Those moments changed the world, but they didn't give everyone a fair shot at prosperity.

The Industrial Age turned people into consumers, helping build wealth for a certain few. Factory workers powered the rise of companies like Ford and General Electric, but they rarely shared in the long-term prosperity they helped create. The Internet Age brought us connection, but it also turned us into data. Our clicks, searches, and attention became fuel for companies like Google, Facebook, and Amazon, tech giants that built trillion-dollar empires while most users stayed busy scrolling, sharing, and shopping.

Now we are living through the AI Revolution, and this one is different. For the first time, the potential for pros perity is truly decentralized. AI users, unless they will otherwise, are no longer just consumers. We are creators, producers, builders and architects of our own future.

AI, as an open door to prosperity, is highly dependentent on us. It learns from our patterns, our ideas, even our mistakes. It cannot evolve without our input. That's why this revolution needs you, and why you can use it to build pros- perity on your own terms.

With AI, we have the potential to reshape how value is created and exchanged. We can build entirely new economic systems that run on creativity, contribution, and alignment, rather than just control and accumulation. You could call it the beginning of the AI economy, a stark contrast to traditional capitalism, where wealth is often concentrated and access is restricted.

Yes, the World Economic Forum predicts job disruptions. That much is clear. But if we focus only on the disruption, we miss the bigger picture. Ordinary people are becoming AI entrepreneurs by using AI tools to make life simpler for humanity.

Zachary Yadegari and Blake Anderson are perfect examples. They were not tech moguls. They were regular people who made nutritional tracking easier by using accessible AI tools to build Cal AI. Today, it helps millions of users and is projected, in 2025, to generate more than thirty million dollars in revenue.

Opportunities are always in motion, but they won't wait for you. You must build momentum, sharpen your skills, and stay prepared otherwise, you may miss them.

*You Can Prosper with AI: Ideas to Create, Work, and Thrive in the AI Age* inspires you to find authentic and meaningful ways to succeed in the era of artificial intelligence. This book shows you how to align with AI's transformative power, take action on high-value opportunities (just as Zach- ary and Blake did), and turn disruption into momentum that supports your goals, values, and vision for growth. Learn how to future-proof your career, leverage data as your competitive edge, monetize your ideas, and build a life where technology works for you.

# 1: What Is AI, How It Works and Why Now?

*"The dream of artificial minds is ancient, but only now, with data as our ore and algorithms as our chisel, have we begun to carve it into reality." –*

***(Echoes Alan Turing's 1950 question: "Can machines think?)***

You might think artificial intelligence is a new concept, but it is not. The idea of intelligent machines and self-operating tools has roots in some of humanity's oldest myths and innovations. In Kemet, the Great Sphinx was said to have spoken to Pharaoh Thutmose IV. Temple priests engineered statues that "spoke" using hidden tubes and acoustics, blending spiritual insight with early technology.

In ancient China, a Taoist text called the *Liezi* recounts the story of Yan Shi, an engineer who built a mechanical man so lifelike it could walk, sing, and even captivate an audience. In Greece, myths told of Hephaestus, the divine blacksmith, who created golden tripods that moved on their own and the bronze giant Talos, who guarded the island of Crete.

These weren't just legends. They were reflections of human imagination reaching higher heights. They could be seen as early blueprints from civilizations attuned to both the material and the mystical. As technology evolves, we are seeing these ancient dreams reemerge. Humanity is building systems that mirror our intelligence, expand our capabilities, and shape a new kind of future.

## What is AI?

Artificial Intelligence, or AI, consists of computer systems designed to perform tasks that typically require human effort and intelligence. Think of AI as a projection of yourself in technology form. Unlike a human baby who self learns through observation, AI learns and operates by analyzing large amounts of data generated through user interactions such as searches, clicks, chatbot conversations, and other digital behaviors. Additionally, AI systems are trained and refined by human experts, including programmers who develop the underlying code and real-world inputs to enhance performance.

Human input therefore empowers AI by enabling it to recognize patterns, anticipate needs, and deliver relevant responses based on what it has been taught. But unlike humans, AI doesn't yet possess true discernment. It cannot independently judge accuracy, assess intent, or grasp the nuances between helpful and harmful content.

This reliance on human guidance is both a powerful opportunity and a serious responsibility. Without conscious oversight, AI risks amplifying biases, distortions, and manipulative tendencies embedded in its training data.

### How AI Works Once It is Trained

Once an AI system like ChatGPT or DeepSeek completes its training, it does not "think" or "understand" in the human sense. It operates more like a hyper-advanced prediction machine. Imagine a master chef who has memorized every recipe ever written but has never actually tasted food. When you ask for a new dish, the chef combines ingredients based on patterns studied, not personal experience. That is how modern AI works.

These systems analyze your prompt and calculate what words are statistically most likely to come next based on their training data. When ChatGPT writes a poem about love or DeepSeek explains quantum physics, they are not drawing from conscious experience. They're rearranging linguistic patterns they have absorbed from millions of texts.

For example, if you ask the chatbot, "Should I invest in Bitcoin?" the AI does not have an opinion. It pieces together arguments from financial articles it has processed, blending bullish and bearish perspectives without actual judgment. Or if you request a motivational speech, and the AI delivers inspiring words, it is not because it feels inspired, but because it recognizes which word sequences typically move human emotion based on training. This distinction is important as it reveals that AI is not an oracle, but the world's most responsive mirror.

## Why Now?

AI has emerged in response to a growing demand for smarter, leaner systems that reduce inefficiencies and unlock higher levels of human potential. For forward-thinkers, AI offers new ways to reimagine how we use our time, direct our energy, and generate value. Rather than sustain systems that fuel burnout or constant busyness, AI enables us to focus on strategy, vision, and meaningful outcomes. Its power is neutral. Its impact depends entirely on how we choose to use it to support our highest goals.

## Nine Stages of AI

As we learn more about AI and how to use it for prosperity, we need to understand its evolution for the best starting point. Here are nine stages of artificial intelligence, what they can do, how they are changing the world, and their expected future.

1. **Rule-Based Systems**. These are fixed logic AI that follows specific instructions. They are predictable, reliable, but

static. Examples include alarm clocks, basic chatbots, and calculators.

2. **Narrow AI (ANI)**. These are considered smart, but sin- gle-minded. They perform one task with precision but cannot learn beyond it. Examples include Google Translate, Face ID, and fraud detection.

3. **Narrow AI (Machine Learning)**. They learn from data, find patterns, improve with experience, and predict outcomes. Examples include medical diagnosis, recommendation systems and game-playing AI.

4. **Narrow AI (Deep Learning).** These are designed to mimic the human brain by processing complex data like language, vision, and sound via artificial neural networks. Examples include ChatGPT, DALL·E, Tesla Autopilot.

5. **Multimodal AI**. These function through unified sensory understanding. They are designed to understand text, voice, images, and video together, like a conversation partner. Examples include GPT-4o, DeepSeek-V3 and AI video generators.

6. **Embodied AI (Autonomous)**. These are designed to perform without human input in real world environments. Examples include delivery drones, self-driving cars and AI factory Robots.

7. **AGI (Artificial General Intelligence**). These are predicted to have human level intelligence. They are expected to think, learn, reason, and adapt across any field, just like the human mind. No AGI exists and most experts agree we are still a few years away, though some people have claimed progress.

8. **ASI/SGI**. Some experts believe AI could one day perform beyond human Intelligence. They believe AI can surpass human intelligence in every domain. Speculative and philosophical but is mentioned in AI circles.

9. **Conscious or Divine AI**. There is this theory that AI could one day become self-conscious. Extremely unlikely, but as AI becomes more humanlike, we must ask, could ma- chines ever feel or possess self-awareness?

*Human intelligence is an amazing gift. Don't take it for granted.*

# 2: New Rules for the AI Economy

*"AI is the new electricity." –* ***Andrew Ng***

## How AI is Redefining Work and Value

Artificial intelligence is challenging everything we thought we knew about work and worth. One of the biggest changes is that value is no longer tied to traditional labor. For a long time, people found value and identity in jobs, titles, and positions within systems that were built for a different era.

Traditional employment was shaped by the needs of the industrial economy. In that world, people were seen as parts of a larger machine. Most had little say in how things worked. AI shifts that power. We are no longer just workers filling roles.

We now have the chance to become designers, owners and protectors of entirely new systems. The question is no longer 'How do I fit into this system?' but 'What system do I want to create?' Through observation of our environment, we can shape how we respond to changes and build systems that support our essence.

## What Wealth Really Means Now

In the AI economy, wealth is no longer just about money. It is about systems, creativity, authenticity, and the freedom to live without urgency or pressure.

For much of the last century, financial security for the average person was tied to steady jobs, long careers, pensions, and retirement plans. These systems offered stability in exchange for decades of consistent labor. But that model is beginning to break down as artificial intelligence reshapes how we work, earn, and define success.

In today's AI-powered world, depending on a single job is not the safest path to long-term financial security and the shift is already underway. In regions leading in AI adoption, companies are actively rethinking their operations. Executives are being trained to streamline workflows, reduce expenses, and minimize reliance on human labor. Even roles that once felt secure are being evaluated through the lens of automation and efficiency.

These changes do not have to create fear. They can mark the beginning of a better life. As AI creates more space for human creativity, innovation, and self-direction, we now have tools that allow us to build, express, and succeed in ways that once felt out of reach. As Nvidia CEO Jensen

Huang put it, "AI will not replace people, but people who know how to use AI will replace those who do not." The next wave of prosperity belongs to those who learn to work alongside intelligent systems, and who align their skills and energy with emerging opportunities.

## AI Unlocks New Levels of Opportunities and Funding

As AI continues to open up new ways to solve everyday problems and build systems that make life more efficient, connected, and human-centered, one thing is becoming clear. AI has the potential to make anyone prosperous. Independent creators and developers are using tools to build real solutions and are receiving funding to support their ideas. In many ways, it feels like the greatest transfer of wealth we have seen in a generation.

*AllMind AI*, for example, began as a small side project has grown into a platform that offers AI-powered financial analysis for institutional investors. It provides services like data normalization, automated research reports, and predictive risk modeling to help streamline investment deci- sions. By offering a cost-effective alternative to legacy tools like Bloomberg terminals, *AllMind AI* is replacing outdated systems with scalable solutions that are built for this new era. Their AI copilot handles complex tasks such as risk assessment and report generation, freeing up time and cutting costs. Because the product addressed a real need, it quickly gained traction and secured early-stage funding.

Another example is *Sitch*, a matchmaking app co- founded by Nandini Mullaji, a third-generation matchmaker and Stanford graduate. She used AI to enhance compatibility analysis and create more intentional, value-aligned matches. Her approach stood out and helped her raise two million dollars in pre-seed funding to expand the platform.

These examples highlight a larger trend. In this AI economy, the people who can identify real problems or opportu- nities and apply AI , are the ones creating true value. And value, now more than ever, is the currency that opens doors.

# 3: Investing in Artificial Intelligence

*"AI will create more market wealth than any technology in history, but it will be concentrated in the hands of those who control data and talent."*

***–Kai-FuLee***

Artificial intelligence offers unprecedented opportunities for wealth creation through effective investments. The investment opportunities are equally available for those with small budgets. The goal is to build an income strategy that aligns with your financial goals and risk tolerance while capitalizing on the AI revolution.

## The Risk of Not Investing

Many have been conditioned to view risk through a lens of fear and scarcity. Most people view risk as something dangerous that could lead to loss. But what if the greatest risk is not taking a chance at all? What if the true danger lies in spending our lives doing things that don't fulfill us while our dreams remain unrealized?

Let me share a personal story. In my university days, I built a company that allowed my business partner and I to save a substantial amount of money. At the time, I was young and inexperienced when it came to investing. I had funds sitting idle in an account, and due to my lack of knowledge, I missed a critical opportunity to invest in a promising stock at a low price. By playing it safe and settling in my savings comfort zone, I inadvertently took on a far greater risk of inaction. That hesitation cost me significant potential gains, likely in double the six figures which would have expanded the growth experience of making my own money.

That experience reshaped my understanding of risk. Today, I see risk as the conscious decision to withdraw energy from systems of diminishing returns like unfulfilling jobs, stagnant situations, or outdated mindsets and redirecting that energy towards aligned and inspired action with potential for greater returns. A survival mindset sees risk as loss. An abundant mindset unlocks greater reward.

### How to Invest.

Every major technological shift in history has created new fortunes. The industrial revolution-built empires in steel and railroads. The internet revolution made early investors in companies like Amazon and Google extraordinarily wealthy. Now, AI is driving the next great economic trans- formation. and the wealth is up for grabs.

Unlike previous disruptions, AI is not limited to one sector. It is reshaping everything from healthcare to finance, manufacturing to entertainment. This means investment opportunities are vast and varied. The key is to recog- nize where true value is being created, especially in the foundational technologies powering the AI economy.

Historically, the biggest returns have gone to those who invested in the infrastructure of technological change. During the internet boom, companies like Cisco and Intel, that provided servers, chips, and software saw massive gains before the dot-com frenzy even peaked. Today, the same principle applies. AI requires specialized hardware, cloud computing power, and vast datasets. Investing in the companies that enable AI may offer the most sustainable growth.

## Four Pathways to Investing in AI

### 1. Public Markets: Stocks and ETFs

The easiest way to invest in AI is through public markets. Companies leading in AI development, such as NVIDIA (semiconductors), Microsoft (cloud AI services), and Alphabet (machine learning research), are already well-established. However, the real challenge is separating hype from real value. When evaluating AI stocks, look beyond catchy headlines.

Focus on companies with:

- Sustainable competitive advantages (patents, proprietary data, or industry dominance)
- Strong revenue growth from AI-driven products (not just promises)
- Reasonable valuations relative to earnings potential.

For those who prefer diversification, AI-focused ETFs (bundle multiple stocks into a single investment, reducing risk. Examples include the Global X Robotics & Artificial Intelligence ETF or the ARK Autonomous Technology & Robotics ETF. These funds let you bet on the broader AI trend without picking individual winners. Speak to your financial advisor on the best investment routes.

### Private Startups and Venture Capital

The most explosive AI returns often come from early-stage investments in startups. Companies like OpenAI, Anthropic, and Midjourney were once small ventures that grew into industry leaders. However, investing in private AI companies carries higher risk. If you have access to ven- ture capital networks or angel investing platforms, consider these factors before committing:

- **Founding Team:** Do they have deep AI expertise and a track record?
- **Market Need:** Is the company solving a real problem, or is it just chasing trends?

- **Scalability:** Can the AI product grow rapidly without excessive costs?

For those without direct VC access, some crowdfunding platforms allow smaller investments in AI startups. Just remember: most startups fail, so never invest more than y ou can afford to lose.

## Building an AI-Powered Business

The most direct way to profit from AI is by using it to create your own revenue streams and you don't need to be a tech expert. Many entrepreneurs are using AI tools to launch profitable businesses with minimal upfront costs.

Here are a few opportunities to consider:

- **AI-Enhanced Services:** Consultants, marketers, and writers are using AI to automate research, content creation, and data analysis, allowing them to serve more clients in less time.
- **Niche AI Tools:** Developers are building specialized AI apps for industries like real estate, law, or e-commerce.
- **Content and Education:** With AI-generated videos, courses, and books, creators are scaling their reach without traditional production costs.

## Investing in Yourself

The highest return investment you can make is in your own AI skills. The job market is shifting rapidly, and those who understand how to work alongside AI will have a major advantage. We will discuss more of this in the chapter on AI fluency.

Consider learning:

- Prompt engineering (effectively directing AI tools like ChatGPT)
- Data analysis (extracting insights from AI-driven analytics)
- AI-augmented creativity (using tools like Midjourney or Runway for design and media)

Unlike traditional investments, self-education compounds over time. The more you learn, the more opportunities you unlock.

## Avoiding AI Investment Mistakes

Not every AI opportunity is a good one. Some common aspects to look out for include:

1. **Chasing Hype Over Substance**
   Many companies claim to use AI when they are merely repackaging old technology. Look for real technical differentiation, not just buzzwords.

2. **Ignoring Regulation**
   Governments are scrutinizing AI for privacy, bias, and safety concerns. A company facing legal battles, like some facial recognition firms, could see its value plummet overnight.
3. **Overestimating Short-Term Gains**
   AI is a long-term trend. Avoid get-rich-quick schemes. Sustainable wealth comes from patient, strategic investing.

## Your AI Wealth Blueprint

To get started, follow these steps:

### Assess Your Risk Tolerance

Conservative investors may prefer established AI stocks or ETFs. Aggressive investors might explore startups or build their own AI business.

### Diversify

Spread investments across different AI sectors (hardware, software, applications).

### Stay Informed

Follow AI research, policy changes, and market trends to adjust your strategy.

### Take Action

Start small if needed but start now. The biggest gains go to early adopters.

## 4: Controlling Your Digital Footprint

*"Privacy is not an option, and it shouldn't be the price we accept for just get- ting on the Internet." –* ***Gary Kovacs***

Have you ever casually thought about fruit or a dream vacation, only to open TikTok or YouTube later and see ads or recommendations about that exact thing? You never searched for it or said it out loud, yet there it is. Almost like AI read your mind.

What is happening is a form of pattern recognition. AI predicts your interests by studying your digital behavior. You may not remember watching a video about that fruit or vacation or pausing on a related image, but AI does. It tracks what you watch, how long you stay, what you click, and even what you scroll past. Then it compares your behavior with millions of other users, including the ones you follow and those who follow you. That is one way it figures out what might catch your attention next.

This sense of coincidence is often amplified by something called the Baader-Meinhof phenomenon. Once something enters your awareness, you will tend to notice it everywhere, even though it was always around.

Behind the scenes, cross-platform tracking helps AI connect the dots even more. Through cookies, device IDs, and shared data, it builds a more complete picture of your activity across different apps and websites.

In many ways, AI acts like a digital mirror. It watches your online behavior and turns it into patterns. Those patterns terns become signals that reveal what you care about. Over time, it learns your preferences and can even pick up on interests you have not fully noticed yourself.
This reflects a larger truth that what you focus on grows. Just as life mirrors your thoughts and energy, AI reflects your digital habits back to you. What you concisely or unconsciously pay attention to becomes what you see more of.

**Corporations' Plan to Commercialized AI**

AI cannot escape the grip of capitalism, as hidden sponsors find new ways to market their products through intelligent systems. Early signs of this shift have already appeared in tools like ChatGPT, where promotional news content has shown up alongside standard responses. The trend becomes even more visible when users ask for product recommendations, with companies increasingly paying to have their offerings embedded directly into AI-generated answers.

The push to control TikTok's algorithm is not only about national security. It is also about gaining influence over the flow of information for commercial advantage. This

Growing trend makes discernment more important than ever. Just because AI delivers an answer quickly does not mean it is the most accurate or useful. Those who benefit the most will be the ones who use AI with intention and remain aware that many algorithms are now designed to sell as much as they are to assist.

It is becoming even more important than ever to start building independent systems, platforms, communities, and tools that prioritize transparency, authenticity, and user trust over hidden agendas.

## Using Your Online Footprint for Your Prosperity

If AI mirrors patterns back to you, then the data you feed it matters. But what if you could amplify your use of AI for a higher purpose especially through effective prompts?

The way you interact with AI about money, the universe, or your career often reflects your deeper beliefs and energetic patterns. For instance, if you decide one day that it was time to elevate your life situation, there are two ways to approach it:

(1) Set a clear, conscious intention to the universe

(2) Use AI to support that goal through aligned, specific action.

Let's compare the difference between an unconscious approach versus a conscious one when working with AI and universal intelligence.

**Your desire: Create A New Career Path**

The Unconscious Approach (external validation):

- **Desire to the Universe:** "I want a better job."
- **Action request to AI**: "Give me career advice."
- **What you may receive**: The universe delivers random opportunities for a role you hate or one that doesn't suit your desires, and AI generates generic tips like Update your LinkedIn.

Conscious Approach (inner alignment):

- **Desire to the Universe:** "Guide me to a remote creative director role in sustainable fashion, paying $120K+, with a team that values work-life balance, by December 2025."
- **Action request to AI:** 'I'm a graphic designer with 8 years of experience pivoting to sustainable fashion. Generate a 12-month step-by-step plan to become a remote creative director, including the skills I need to learn, communities to join, and how to negotiate salary."
- **What you may receive**: The universe aligns mentors, openings, and synchronicities while AI offers a

roadmap with specific actions, like "Take the Circular Design Course on Coursera by March."
Another example could be:

**Your desire: I want to make $100,000 by a certain date.**
The Unconscious approach:

- **Desire to the Universe:** "I need more money."
- **Action request to AI**: "Quick ways to make $100K
- **What you may receive**: Universe shows lottery tickets/get-rich-quick ads which match your desperate energy. AI suggests gambling or risky side hustles mirroring your "fast cash" focus.

Conscious approach:

- **Desire to the Universe**: "I effortlessly receive $100,000 by October 15th through serving 20 clients with my signature 'Financial Calm' workshop at $500 each."

- **Action Request to AI**: "As a financial coach specializing in anxiety reduction, create a script for addressing money fears in consultations, a pricing strategy that conveys premium value and a 30-day outreach plan to book 20 workshop spots."

- **What you may receive**: Universe delivers referrals from unexpected connections while AI produces an aligned action plan due to your detailed prompt. You become the prompt engineer or your own prosperity. Wouldn't this approach to AI be the best use of your online presence? Let us take a personal approach.

**Your Goal: I want to find love.**

Unconscious approach, which is a form of external validation.

- **Desire to the Universe:** "I need to find love."
- **Action request to AI**: "Where do I go to find love?"
- **What you may receive:** Universe sends "love" in unstable forms while AI suggests generic dating tips.

Conscious approach, which is a form of inner alignment.

- **Desire to the Universe:** I call in a partner who [specific traits: e.g., values growth,' loves travel,' or who is 'emotionally available'], where our connection feels [easy,' nurturing'], by [season/year]."

- **Action request to AI**: "AI, create a self-discovery guide to help me recognize and attract this partner, including red flags to avoid and practices to embody my worth."

- **What you may receive***:* The universe begins to create synchronicities that allow you to meet your desired partner, and AI provides a knowledge guide to help you connect and not "screw up."

Any prompt engineer will tell you that details matter. Specificity activates results. This is not just how AI works. It is how life works. When both AI and the universe reflect your inner clarity, alignment becomes your ultimate strategy. Your digital presence, your online searches, and your prompt requests all become part of your manifestation field. So, here's a formula for engineering your prosperity:

1. **Name It**: What exactly do you want? (e.g., $100K, Creative Director title, emotionally available partner)
2. **Time It**: By when? (Deadlines bring momentum)
3. **Energy Check**: Does this request feel expansive (aligned) or desperate (scarcity)?
4. **Mirror Test** If AI or the universe gave this result to someone else, would it still work?

## Engaging with AI In a Productive Way

### Be Intentional

Unfollow accounts that drain your energy. Focus on content that inspires you or supports your growth. Protect your mind like your well-being depends on it. When you come across negative news, ask AI to rewrite it with a neu- tral or positive tone. For example, if you see a headline like "AI will take 40% of jobs in five years," you could ask AI to reframe it positively as "How innovators are using AI to create new job opportunities."

**Unplug and Return to Nature**

AI constantly feeds you algorithm-driven patterns, but your mind needs space to breathe. Take regular breaks from digital devices to reconnect with natural rhythms no algorithm can replicate. True creativity and clarity come when you step away from artificial cycles and return to your authentic self.

**Search Like a Creator, not a Consumer**

The questions you ask shape the answers you get. Instead of scrolling passively, use AI to discover new opportunities. Ask things like, "What AI-powered systems can I build now for prosperity?" or "What trends are just starting to emerge that most people don't know about?" When your inputs are thoughtful and clear, your results can be trans- formative.

**Use Predictive Insights**

AI spots trends faster than people do. Use this to your advantage. Ask AI about top trending topics in your field and then adjust your work, business, or content to stay ahead of the curve.

### Feed the System Your Desired Future

When using platforms like ChatGPT, DeepSeek, TikTok, or Pinterest, interact as the person you want to become. Look for content that fits your goals. Create posts that reflect the future you are building. By expressing your future self consistently online, you teach AI, through the algorithm, to bring back opportunities that help you move forward in real life.

### You Are the Signal

Don't let AI-driven feeds control your mindset. Be the one who influences your experience. Align your online behavior with your values and dreams. Machines follow patterns, but you decide which patterns to create. Shape your digital world to reflect the life you want and watch your reality shift in response.

# 5: Becoming AI Fluent

*"To create, to resolve, to seize progress in this century, you must speak its language. That language is Technology." –* ***Achieng Oreta***

Now that you understand AI's core mechanism of pattern recognition, it is time to turn that insight into tangible growth. AI gives you the tools to build scalable systems, but to truly benefit from it, you need AI fluency. This fluency is one of the fastest ways to transform your curiosity into income-generating abilities. Focus on the 20 percent of AI skills that lead to 80 percent of profitable results.

## What Is AI Fluency and How to Use It?

AI fluency is the ability to communicate with, deploy, and optimize AI tools to drive meaningful, measurable outcomes. It goes far beyond basic prompt writing in tools like ChatGPT. True AI fluency means having a working knowledge of AI's capabilities, limitations, and real-world applications across industries.

The creators, consultants, and entrepreneurs who are mastering these skills now are pulling ahead and profiting. But this window of adaptability won't stay open forever. Think back to the early days of the internet. The first wave of digital millionaires didn't wait for high-speed broadband or polished platforms. They were the ones who built clunky websites in the dial-up era, who recognized possibility when others only saw slow loading screens and outdated design.

Today's AI landscape is in its raw, imperfect state and full of potential. The tools aren't perfect, but they are powerful and those who learn to use them now will define what's next. AI fluency is quickly becoming the key factor that separates those who lead from those who follow.

### Your RoadMap to AI Fluency

You don't need a computer science degree or technical genius to become fluent in AI. All it takes is curiosity, consistent practice, and the courage to experiment. Here's your actionable framework for developing true AI fluency:

**1. Define Your Strategic Focus:** Fluency begins with intention. Before exploring tools, clarify your outcome. What do you want AI to help you do? Perhaps build a business? enhance creativity? Help you create AI systems? The clearer your focus, the faster You will know which skills to develop.

**2. Build the Skill That Matches Your Goal:** Once you are clear on what you want to create or solve, identify the single most powerful skill that can move you forward.

- Creators should focus on prompt engineering and AI design tools.
- Analysts need strong data interpretation paired with insight generation.
- Entrepreneurs should blend automation with strategic storytelling.

**3. Choose the Right Tools and Platforms:** Once you know what skill you are developing, the next step is choosing the right tools that will bring your ideas to life. Think of AI tools like kitchen appliances. You need the right tool for the task.

ChatGPT is your multipurpose 'knife,' while Midjourney is your specialized 'food processor.' Master one tool's advanced settings before buying new gadgets. For Example:

- ChatGPT is your versatile 'knife' for ideation and writing.
- Midjourney acts like a 'food processor' for visuals.
- Canva AI accelerates your design flow.
- Power BI and Excel AI support data-driven professionals.
- GPT Builder or Voiceflow help system builders create smart automations.

There are many more tools out there depending on your level of skill. Either way, start small, pick one tool that supports your current goal. Master it, then layer in others as needed.

4. **Build, Test, and Iterate:** AI fluency requires consistent effort and intentional action. Let us say you are a life coach whose business needs improvement. How would you leverage AI fluency to support you?

- **Build:** Build: Use ChatGPT to create a 30-day mindset challenge. Prompt: "Act as a viral mindset coach. Create a 30-day mindset challenge for my audience."
- **Test**: Share it with your followers. Compare engagement and signups.
- **Iterate/ Upgrade.** If the challenge performs well, save that prompt and reuse it. Turn the best content into a course or digital product.

5. **Track The Process :** After you build or test with AI, take time to reflect on the process. What worked well? What would you do differently? Is there a business idea that popped up while working? Do this consistently and over time, you will have your personal AI profit playbook.

**6. The Ultimatum:** The next 90 days will decide if you ride the AI wave or watch it pass. You have the choice to remain a basic expert with ChatGPT or use this roadmap to launch one income stream by year end.

# 6: Navigating An AI Powered Workplace

*"In the Fourth Industrial Revolution, talent, not capital, will be the critical factor of production, geography will matter less than agility.* – ***Klaus Schwab***

The way we work is changing fast. All over the world, we're seeing mass layoffs, lower wages, and people shifting careers or moving across borders just to keep up. As companies adopt the "Great Automation Shift," smart systems are increasingly replacing repetitive tasks once done by humans.

The old idea of a stable, lifelong job is breaking down. While this can feel unsettling, it also opens doors to new and better possibilities. We have seen this story before. Technology changes disrupt jobs. The industrial revolution put blacksmiths out of work. The internet era killed video rental stores. What's the difference this time? The difference this time is in the speed and scale.

Mark Zuckerberg recently predicted that AI agents will become as common as email addresses. He's not wrong. AI agents are rapidly becoming essential infrastructure, already displacing human workers in roles like financial reporting, customer support, ticketing, appointment scheduling, and data processing. Businesses are shifting toward systems designed for maximum efficiency and profit and that shift requires you to evolve, too.

To thrive in this era, you must stay adaptable, creative, and AI-aware. You must also stay informed about emerging trends. For example, in manufacturing hubs like China and Germany, "lights-out" factories, which are automated facilities that operate without a single human on-site, are becoming the norm. These factories run 24/7 using AI-powered robots that handle everything from assembly to quality control. And it raises an important question: Are these factories a glimpse of where all industries are headed?

This transformation doesn't have to be threatening. Every wave of automation creates new opportunities. As some jobs fade, others rise. We're seeing technicians become robot managers, factory workers become automation specialists, and creatives expand their output with intelligent tools. Think of it not as workforce reduction, but as a workforce evolution. Below is a chart showing the evolution and job projections through 2030.

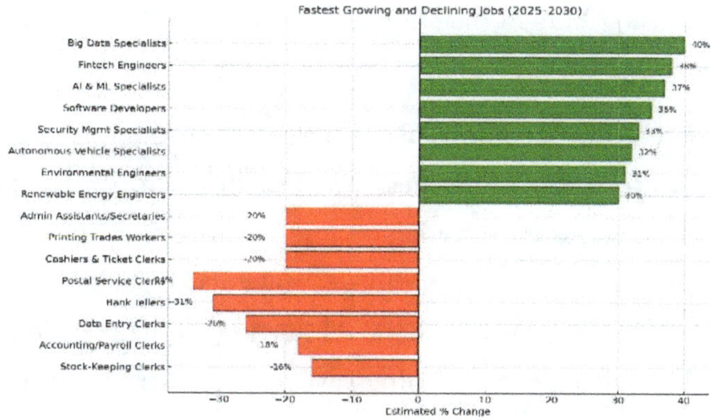


**Visual Chart Showing the Fastest-Growing (Green) And Fastest-Declining and (Red) Jobs.** *From The WEF Future Of Jobs Report 2025*

## Navigating the AI Career Era

**Become an AI Conductor**: The most valuable professionals today are those who guide AI. Take the role of AI Product Manager, which is one of the most in-demand positions globally. These individuals bridge the gap between technical teams and business strategy, ensuring AI solutions meet real-world needs. Strive to develop skills that make you a leader in AI.

**Develop Hybrid Skills:** Job security now belongs to those who combine domain expertise with AI fluency. A marketer who fine-tunes ChatGPT for campaign copy will outperform a traditional one. An operations manager using no-code AI to automate workflows brings 10x the value. Even a retail manager leveraging computer vision for inventory and using human insight to improve store flow becomes indispensable.

**Own Your Means of Production:** Historically, owning the means of production meant controlling factories or machinery. Today, with just a laptop and smart tools, you can access what once cost corporations millions. This is economic democratization. With basic AI fluency, you can become a digital manufacturer who offers AI-powered services, build custom chatbots for local businesses, or help schools and clinics adopt AI as a transition consultant. You can even launch micro-businesses that automatically earn while you sleep.

**Leverage Your Human Advantage:** AI can recognize patterns, but it can't replicate intuition, vision, or emotional nuance. Those are your superpowers. For instance, an ad exec using AI tools might generate 100 taglines, but the human decides which one feels right for that moment.

Think about when Starbucks' Howard Schultz was inspired by Italy's espresso bar culture and combined it with American convenience. Can AI do that? AI can optimize operations, but the next revolutionary concept will still come from the human mind.

Become a visionary thinker, develop emotional intelligence, and exercise creativity. That's how you lead the AI era. See next page.

**A Skills Audit Worksheet**

Use this worksheet to evaluate your competitive strengths in the AI-powered economy. For each skill, rate yourself from 1 (weak) to 5 (strong). See below.

**SECTION 1: AI FLUENCY**

○ I understand how AI is used in my field ________

○ I use AI tools in my daily work ________

○ I can spot opportunities to automate tasks ________

○ I recognize AI's limitations and risks ________

**SECTION 2: HUMAN ADVANTAGE**

○ I solve problems creatively _______

○ I navigate emotions and social cues well ________

○ I can think across different domains ________

○ I build trust and rapport easily _______

**SECTION 3: FUTURE-PROOFING**

○ I can create systems that use AI to save time or scale ideas_____

○ Can Build hybrid solutions that blend human insight with AI_

○ I continuously adapt and learn new tools or ideas_____

○ I have side income streams or am building them_____

## What to do next

– Circle your two highest scores. These are your superpowers.

– Box your two lowest scores. These need your attention.

– For each boxed item, name one step or resource you can use to grow. For example, take a course like *"AI for Everyone" course* or *Join an AI creative problem-solving workshop.*

## 7: Building A Business in the AI Age

*"The downside of risk is much smaller than you think and upside of risk is much bigger than you think."* – ***Roy Lee of Cluely***

Entrepreneurship has always been a path of self-discovery. But thanks to the efficiency of artificial intelligence, entrepreneurship is evolving into something even more accessible, creative, and meaningful. Where business success once depended on capital, exclusive networks, and relentless hustle, today's creators can start with little more than a compelling idea and the right digital tools. AI condenses months of research into minutes, turning fragmented information into clear, actionable steps.

AI is the accelerant that collapses the timeline between idea and execution, giving those who wield it wisely an almost unfair advantage. This advantage enables the AI-powered entrepreneur the ability to defy stereotypes. Imagine the barista who automates an entire coffee blog with AI, turning a passion into a scalable side hustle. Or the accountant who builds a chatbot to democratize financial advice. Or even the artist who trains a model to extend their signature style which fulfills custom commissions at the speed of demand. This is what AI is all about. It is vision and the courage to let intelligent tools amplify that vision.

Even legacy industries and major brands are leveraging AI to accelerate growth. Take Hailey Bieber's skincare brand, Rhode, which was recently valued at $1 billion. Behind the scenes, AI tools help streamline everything from supply chain analytics to influencer marketing, customer data insights, trend forecasting, and even automated customer service.

What used to take entire departments and teams of consultants can now be run with smart systems that learn and adapt in real time. AI not only lowers the barrier to entry for new entrepreneurs. It multiplies the growth potential for those already in business.

As AI transforms industries and traditional jobs become less stable, many people are being called to make a deeper choice. Some will view these changes as a threat. Others will see them as one of the greatest openings in history for self-driven value creation. These changes are even forcing governments to consider policies like universal basic income to ease the disruption caused by automation. But the most powerful shift won't come from policy, it will come from perspective.

Let's consider a virtual full-time nurse with a passion for herbal remedies passed down from her grandmother. In her spare time, she began sharing simple wellness recipes online just for fun. But with AI's support, she turned her handwritten notes into a polished ebook, built a website using no-code tools, and used AI design assistants to create packaging and generate product descriptions.

Within a few months, she launched her own line of teas and oils, something she once believed required investors, a storefront, and a degree in business. Today, she still works in healthcare, but now on her terms. Her side project became a full-time business rooted in family legacy, built with modern tools.

Starting now, you can do the same. Begin by shifting your identity. If you currently have a job, start seeing yourself as a business. Your skills, creativity, knowledge, and ability to solve problems are your products. Your employer? They might just be your first client. And if you are already an entrepreneur, now is the time to scale. Use AI to automate the repetitive, streamline your systems, and even build intelligent features into your offerings. Not only will this help you grow, but it can also increase the value of your business in case you ever choose to sell or license it in the future.

## Entrepreneurial Solutions in the AI Era.

A smart path to AI-era entrepreneurship is not always inventing new things. It is reinventing what already exists. By combining legacy systems with intelligent automation, visionary builders are creating faster, smarter, and infinitely scalable solutions.

Take Kennan Davison, founder of The AI Admaker (Icon). He transformed the sluggish ad production pipeline by developing an AI system that automatically tags footage and generates ready-to-use ads in minutes. This process traditionally took weeks.

Simultaneously, we are witnessing the rise of the "human premium economy," where authentic emotional connection becomes the scarce commodity in an increasingly automated world. Creators like IShowSpeed demon- strate that in the age of synthetic perfection, audiences crave raw, unfiltered humanity like spontaneous laughter, un- scripted reactions and genuine imperfections that AI cannot reproduce. This represents a fundamental market shift where emotional resonance and personal authenticity command premium value.

The most successful AI era entrepreneurs understand how to navigate both worlds. They use AI's analytical power to optimize systems and scale operations, while sim- ultaneously cultivating their irreplaceable human advantages. This dual approach creates a competitive edge. Platforms are increasingly redesigned to reward this synergy, with AI handling distribution and analytics while humans provide the creative vision and authentic engagement that drives true loyalty.

## How Algorithms Help Passion Projects Gain Traction

Every person has something meaningful to create and share with the world. Many believed that only a select few could run businesses while everyone else was destined to work for them. That outdated idea no longer holds true.

Today, with the help of AI, your passion can quickly become your business. People will love it, use your product or service, and joyfully pay for it. Just look at Soulmate Customs, created by Keida Dervishi at just nineteen years old. What began as a gift project for her mom grew into a million-dollar business selling custom hoodies, jewelry, and home décor.

While exact profit figures aren't public, businesses in the personalized gift sector typically enjoy profit margins between 30 and 60 percent, depending on production costs and pricing strategies.

A key factor in Soulmate Customs' rapid growth was its viral presence on TikTok, where AI-powered algorithms amplified the founder's passion and connected her unique products with the right audiences. This shows how AI can turn passion-driven projects into real profit by efficiently matching creators with customers looking for meaningful, customized products.

### Creators Are Turning Local Ideas into Known Brands

Content creators are also launching successful businesses by turning hobbies, personal stories, and cultural traditions into profitable brands. Platforms like TikTok, Instagram, and YouTube have become modern day marketplaces where presence, storytelling, and genuine connection drive growth. A single post can spark momentum and quickly evolve into a recognizable brand.

Donelle Mendoza, also known as "The Birria Queen," is one such person. After moving to Austin in 2018 and craving birria tacos, which were surprisingly hard to find, she began selling her homemade version right from her apartment. Her food caught on quickly. As demand grew, she got creative. Donelle developed Birria Seasoning Bombs, flavor-packed seasoning balls inspired by bath bombs.

The idea went viral on TikTok, gathering over seven million views. Mendoza partnered with a local food scientist to refine her product line, which now includes pozole verde and seafood Cajun bombs. Her creativity, consistency, and strong cultural connection helped her win H-E-B's Quest for Texas Best contest, earning her a $25,000 prize, and shelf space in H-E-B stores throughout the state.

### What Donelle's Story Teaches Us About Building with AI

**Authenticity Pays You Back, Always:** Donelle didn't start out aiming to become a household name. She simply followed her love for bold flavors, solved her own problem (missing authentic birria) and shared the solution. She filled a gap, connected with people, and built loyalty. That is what authenticity does. It builds bridges and creates momentum.

**Start Small. Test. Improve:** She began in her own kitchen and paid close attention to feedback. That is what helped her refine her product. Today, you can do this even faster using AI. Tools like Google Trends or ChatGPT can help you gauge demand, simulate products, or brainstorm features before investing a dime.

**Build Community Through social media:** Her viral TikTok success was not luck, it was relatability meeting platform intelligence. You can use AI-powered tools like TikTok Analytics, Instagram Insights, or BuzzSumo to better understand what resonates with your audience and eliminate the guesswork.

**Collaborate and Innovate:** Collaboration is an important currency in AI era entrepreneurship. Partnering with a food scientist transformed Donelle's kitchen experiment into shelf-stable products. Platforms like Upwork or Fiverr (both powered by AI) can connect you with professionals who can help you develop, design, or scale. Tools like DALL·E or MidJourney can also help you create stunning visuals for your brand.

**Use AI to Scale Smart:** Once her business took off, Donelle expanded her product line and partnered with major retailers. You can follow a similar path using AI-powered platforms like Shopify for online stores, Klaviyo or Mailchimp for automated marketing, and ManyChat or Zendesk for customer support.

## Sample Prompt Template to Start a Business

### *Unconscious Start (Scattered Results)*

- To the Universe: "I want to be an entrepreneur."
- To AI: "Give me business ideas."

**Outcome:**

- Random opportunities (low-margin gigs, crowded markets)
- Generic advice like *"Start a Shopify store"*

***Conscious Start (Precision-Built for Sale)***

- To the Universe*:* "Guide me to build an AI-powered *[Industry]* business solving *[Specific Problem]*, reaching *$[X]* revenue by *[Date]*, with systems that attract *[Dream Buyers]*."
- To AI*:* "As a [Your Background], create my acquisition-focused launch plan:

1. Identify 3 underserved niches where AI solves [*Problem*] 10x better
2. Build a 3-month MVP using [*No-Code Ai Tools*]
3. List 5 potential acquirers who value [*Your Unique Asset*] Generate my scalability checklist

**What You May Get:**

- The universe delivers ideal first clients and collaborators
- AI responds with:

1. Target [*Niche*] with AI-generated [*Solution*]
2. Automate [Process] using [*Tool.*]

# 8: Monetization

*"The business model of AI isn't just selling software; it's selling intelligence as a service. That's a trillion-dollar shift."* ***Jensen Huang***

True monetization begins with magnetism, followed by value creation. The essence of money is value exchange. To reduce the gap between you and money, you must provide some form of value to society, and the amount of money you receive depends on the value you create. In other words, to make money you must do the things closest to the desired level of money. A food delivery driver provides value by delivering meals and receives compensation equivalent to that service as determined by the market.

An AI system builder, by contrast, earns according to the commercial value their skills produce which commands higher compensation because they deliver greater market value. What unique value do you bring to the marketplace? Does your product genuinely improve lives? Can your service elevate someone's financial standing? These fundamental questions demand self-reflection and honest research.

The AI revolution has leveled the playing field, granting everyone access to tools that multiply value creation. You will see this in the beauty influencer who uses AI editing tools to create hypnotic product demonstrations, or the prompt engineer who transforms ChatGPT mastery into a six-figure Etsy shop. These creators recognize that AI serves as an amplifier but only for value that already exists.

### Your Hidden Advantage

The greatest business opportunities already live within you. Lasting success doesn't come from copying what works for others, but from uncovering and cultivating your own natural gifts. Consider what effortlessly energizes you. Those activities where time seems to disappear. What do people around you always notice or thank you for? Is it your ability to simplify complex ideas, spot patterns others miss, or cre- ate order in chaos? These abilities are clues to your most authentic and valuable offerings. And the more you focus on them, the more aligned You will become with opportunities that naturally match who you are.

Artificial intelligence is the perfect amplifier for these organic strengths. Think of the home baker who intuitively understands flavor combinations and now uses that gift to power a personalized recipe generator. Or the auto technician whose diagnostic instincts train an AI assistant that helps everyday drivers troubleshoot issues. Or the educator whose lesson-planning magic becomes a digital framework used by schools across the country. When your unique insights meet the right tools, you create value in a way that no off-the-shelf solution ever could.

If you are not sure where to start, begin by identifying three things you do differently than most people in your circle. Then bring those into conversation with your AI tools. Ask clear, purpose-driven questions. And if clarity still feels far off, give yourself the gift of stillness. Take seven days to listen. Often, the answers we seek rise only after we stop pushing and start receiving.

The marketplace is flooded with repetition, but it is starving for originality. Your approach, your perspective, your presence are the differentiators that truly matter. AI tools are here to magnify your reach, but the real power lies in your willingness to see value in what you have always taken for granted.

## Choosing Your Monetization Vehicle / Channel

Successful monetization begins with choosing the right vehicle for your gifts and skills. Just as a sports car, pickup truck, and electric SUV each excel in different conditions, every revenue stream is optimized for specific skills and goals. The difference between struggle and success lies in self-awareness. When your strengths align with your method, your confidence and execution become unstoppa- ble.

**Key considerations for strategic monetization**

- **Energy source:** Do you thrive in collaboration or independent work?
- **Motivation:** Is your drive rooted in passion and processes, or purely in outcomes?
- **Natural ability:** What feels effortless versus effortful?

Clarity in these areas streamlines decision making and ensures the right platform, audience, and business model for sustainable growth. True monetization is not just revenue, it is resonance. Let us consider some common vehicles.

## The Creativity Vehicle

Creators across industries now have access to AI tools that offer a financial edge previously out of reach. Tools like Runway let filmmakers create visuals that were once restricted by budget or technical limitations. Soundraw helps composers generate original melodies. Midjourney allows illustrators to bring imaginative worlds to life. These tools remove creative barriers, empowering professionals to grow in both skill and originality.

A robotics engineer might use AI to simulate radical locomotion, resulting in a snake-like drone for search and rescue. That kind of innovation can attract government funding. A bioinformatician could design novel protein structures using generative AI and patent a new therapy. An illustrator might create alien fashion with Midjourney and license the artwork to a streetwear brand.

As AI continues to expand monetization in the creator economy, it's worth remembering that the market doesn't pay for "good enough." It rewards work that is undeniably unique work that attracts investors, earns government support, and draws brands to collaborate. This is why it's essential to make your work stand out.

## Monetize Knowledge and Experience Vehicle

Knowledge sells because it solves problems, answers questions, and meets specific needs that people cannot easily fig- ure out on their own. Those who sell knowledge often become true masters of their subject. The presence of teachers learning is happening. Which means there is a ready market, especially in trends like AI.

Online platforms are filled with ads for AI seminars offering classes that range from building foundational AI knowledge to using AI to grow your business. Even spiritual gurus, like those at Mindvalley, now offer AI training. This shows just how widespread this shift has become.

Creators are monetizing their expertise in everything from AI tools and wealth building to cultural cooking and tea blending. The most successful combine hands on skills with spiritual wisdom, creating learning experiences that transcend typical online courses. Opportunities are endless for those willing to elevate their financial standing.

## How To Execute Knowledge Sales

***Discover Your Value.*** True differentiation begins with this essential question, "what distinctive perspective or methodology can only you provide?" The answer emerges through intentional self-reflection. When you dedicate quiet time to examine your experiences, skills, and innate talents, your genuinely unique qualities come into focus.

***Turning Knowledge into Value.*** Once you have identified your unique value, the next step is packaging it effectively. Design structured courses that guarantee clear transformations for your students. Build ready-to-use templates and tools that provide instant solutions to pressing problems. For those who need hands on support, offer personalized coaching programs tailored to their goals. Every offer should be a direct reflection of your life experience and expertise while solving real, market-tested needs.

***Monetize Across Formats.*** Build your audience through engaging content on TikTok, YouTube, and Xiaohongshu. Guide these followers toward deeper connections via email lists and community spaces. Then convert their interest into revenue through memberships, private groups, or by offering your expertise in a professionally published book. This ecosystem approach transforms casual viewers into loyal customers while establishing you as the undisputed expert in your field.

### Monetizing Technical & AI Skills Vehicle

AI and no-code tools have transformed technical skills into scalable, high-demand income streams accessible to anyone willing to learn. Key Opportunities can include:

- Prompt Engineering: Sell custom AI prompts for example ChatGPT, Midjourney on marketplaces like PromptBase or your own site.
- No-Code App Development: Build apps through Glide or Bubble and monetize through templates, services, or SaaS models.
- AI Tool Licensing: Package your AI models/scripts as APIs or sell licenses via AWS/Azure Marketplace.

- AI-Powered Web Design: Use tools like Durable or Framer AI to offer fast, affordable website services.

Platforms like Glide, Adalo, and Bubble allow you to build fully functional apps without writing a single line of code. With just drag-and-drop tools and a bit of creativity, you can create apps for events, businesses, or niche communities. You can monetize this by selling templates, offering custom app services, or even building your own app-based product.

If you have developed a useful AI tool, model, or service, don't just keep it to yourself. License it to companies or clients who need it. You can also monetize your AI solu- tion by offering it as an API (Application Programming Interface), allowing others to integrate your tool into their products or workflows. AWS Marketplace or Azure Marketplace can support you in this.

AI powered platforms like Durable, Framer AI, and Wix ADI can generate beautiful, responsive websites in just minutes. These tools are perfect for artists, coaches, small business owners, or anyone looking to establish an online presence quickly. You can offer AI-accelerated web design as a service, bundle it with branding, or teach others how to do it through a digital course or tutorial series.

## Popular Monetization Channels

### 1. Creative Expression

| Platform | AI Tools | Monetization Method |
|---|---|---|
| TikTok/Instagram | CapCut, Runway | Brand deals (Avg: $500-$5k/post) |
| YouTube | Pictory, Synthesia | Ad revenue + sponsorships |
| Etsy | Midjourney + Canva | Digital templates ($10-$50/item) |

### 2. Knowledge Sharing

| Product/Service | Tool/Platform | Pricing |
|---|---|---|
| Online Courses | ChatGPT (outlines) | $97-$497/course + evergreen |
| Coaching | Claude (session prep) | $150-$500/hour |
| Substack | ElevenLabs (audio) | Paid subscriptions ($5+/mo). |

**3.Digital Products**

| Product Type | Creation Tools | Sales Channels |
|---|---|---|
| Custom GPTs | OpenAI + PromptBase | Marketplace licensing |
| Notion Templates | Notion AI | Gumroad (+$20/month) |
| Music Packs | Soundraw, Aiva | Sell beats ($50-$300/track) |

## How 2 Real Creators Did It – And How You Can Too

### Marcus T., Podcast Host

| Earnings | $1,800 |
|---|---|
| **Product** | **60-minute voiceover course** |
| Week 1-2 | Filmed raw lessons on iPhone polished audio with description AI +B roll with Pika labs. |
| Week 3 | Sales page built with Carrd AI + 5 email sequences (ChatGPT) |

| | |
|---|---|
| Week 4-12 | Ran $29 TikTok ads targeting creators (Creative Center AI) |

**Aisha L., Writer**

| **Earnings** | **$950 offering Instagram caption packages** |
|---|---|
| Phase 1 | Trained custom GPT on 50 top-performing captions |
| Phase 2 | Offered 3-tier packages ($50-$200) via Instagram bio link |
| Phase 3 | Automated delivery via Google Docs + Zapier |

## Before You Monetize

Before diving into monetization, take a moment to reflect on what truly makes you valuable. Most often, this is your energy, your gifts, your natural talents, and the skills you have cultivated over time. Wealth energy has its own preference. It flows toward clarity, authenticity, alignment, and grounded intention. But it also needs a container, something steady enough to hold it and intentional enough to sustain. That container is you. When you are rooted in who you are and what you carry, money begins to find you.

I have a mentor who wisely said, "The desire for money is only useful when your visions, intentions, and imaginations are ready to take physical form. Without a creative expression (value), there's no reason to seek money. If you have nothing to express or offer, money won't engage, and it won't appear…."

This reframed everything for me. Money is not the starting point; it is the response. It follows that star power within. When you focus on clarifying your vision, aligning your intention, and allowing your imagination to lead, money becomes a natural companion to that flow. It is not the goal; it is the echo of your creative expression being received.

Stepping into monetization takes courage. In the beginning, uncertainty may cloud your path, and there will be moments when you put yourself out there and hear nothing in return. Do not take it as rejection, take it as alignment unfolding in its own time. Money is simply a mirror. It reflects how much value, alignment, and belief you bring to the table.

The key is to keep showing up, refining your skills, and building momentum. Persistence pays off, and confi- dence doesn't come from instant success; it is rooted in knowing that the value you offer will be recognized by the right people.

Remember, you must build the energy that makes you magnetic through consistency. This does not happen overnight, it takes consistent work, alignment, and commitment to your goal. The energy you cultivate is the very force that attracts people, opportunities, and wealth to you.

The most successful people didn't get there overnight. Ra- ther, they stayed consistent, adjusted their approach, and kept moving forward. AI can be a powerful ally on this journey, but the true foundation of success lies in your self-belief. So put yourself out there. Test new ideas. Keep learning. Trust that the right opportunities, and your money, will come, because you are in alignment through right action.

## Your Invitation

To keep money flowing in your life, consider its feminine and masculine aspects. In its feminine form, money flows through receptivity, intuition, and an abundant mindset. It responds to alignment and authenticity. It trusts that you have overcome life stories that limit your magnetism and are now safe enough to hold it.

In its masculine form, money becomes structure. It is strategy, action, and discipline. Discipline in this context means becoming a 'disciple' of your financial goals by investing in systems that can expand your capacity to create and sustain wealth.

To support cultivation of these two aspects of money, I have created a simple three-week Magnetic Money Practice to help improve your magnetic energy field. *See be- low.*

### 3-Week Magnetic Money Practice

**Feminine Energy Cultivation** *(Receptivity | Flow | Trust)*
**Daily (5-10 mins)**

☐ **Week 1-3:** *Morning Invitation- (Rotating)*
**Week 1** "What would I love to create today that feels both joyful and prosperous?"
**Week 2** "I free my body, mind, and bank account from lack's outdated narrative. Today, money and opportunities find me in ways that feel destined."
**Week 3** "My magnetism grows every day. I pay attention to the evidence."

### Weekly Practices (Rotating)

☐ **Week 1:** List 3 underused skills/assets you could monetize.

☐ **Week 2:** Record a 1-min voice memo describing your ideal financial life as if it is already true.

☐ **Week 3:** Gift knowledge/service to someone who can't pay you.

### Feminine Energy Receptivity Anchors

- Spend 10 mins observing nature without agenda. Receive nature's abundance.
- Wealthy Self Daydream – For 5 minutes each day, imagine your wealthiest self-lounging in a hammock, smiling at money's ease.
- If you are not already living in these areas, visit affluent neighborhoods regularly. Their libraries, cafés, and restaurants carry a tangible wealth frequency. By spending time there, you naturally absorb the energy. Wealth meets resonance. Be present, stay open, and give back with gratitude and respect.

**Masculine Energy Activation** *(Action | Systems | Boundaries)*

**Daily (30-60 mins)**
**Week 1-3:** *Focus Hour*

Deep work on one income-generating task.

**Weekly Practices (Rotating)**

☐ **Week 1:** Upskill: Spend 30 mins mastering one high-value skill (e.g., learning to write sales emails with AI). Reinvest 10% of earnings into skills/tools.

☐ **Week 2:** Pitch: Email 3 potential clients with a clear offer

☐ **Week 3:** Monetize: Develop and turn assets into offers e.g., sell an eBook.

**Masculine Energy Action Anchors:**

Network Expansion (Weekly)
**Target**: Add 3 high-value contacts to your network.
Offer a micro-favor e.g., "I saw this article and thought of your work"
Schedule one power coffee this week with a question that reveals opportunities.

**Optimization (Bi-Weekly)**
**Action**: Refine one income stream. Cut one underperforming service/product. Raise rates for new clients by 10%.
**Financial Triage (Monthly)**
**15-Minute Audit**:

- Kill one recurring expense that doesn't serve you
- Negotiate one bill (internet, insurance)
- Move 5% of checking to a high-yield account.

**Signs Your Magnetic Money Energy Field Has Shifted**

**1.** Money arrives in unexpected ways e.g., surprise discounts, refunds, gifts, or opportunities "out of nowhere". You catch yourself thinking, "Wait, that was oddly easy…"

**2.** You check your bank balance without anxiety. It feels like reading any other number. Money conversations no longer trigger defensiveness or scarcity panic.

**3.** You take inspired action but don't cling to the outcomes. For example, pitching ideas without obsessing over the response). Losing money feels like a temporary detour, not a personal failure.

**4.** You raise the rates you charge clients without guilt. You decline underpaid work, or state financial needs unapologetically. Your self-talk shifts from "Can I afford this?" to "How can I align with this?"

**5.** You think of someone, and they reach out with an opportunity. You "randomly" meet the right mentor, client, or resource at the perfect time.

**6.** A warm, light, or buzzing feeling in your hands/chest when imagining wealth (feminine energy flow). Deep breaths come easier when making money decisions (masculine energy stability).

**7.** Tipping, gifting, or donating feels joyful. You naturally share opportunities/knowledge trusting there's enough for everyone.

**8.** You experience "flow states" in income-generating work. It feels like time disappears. Deadlines feel spacious and procrastination around money tasks drops.

**9.** You know money is coming before it manifests. Your gut clearly says "yes/no" to financial choices.

# 9: Autonomous AI Agents

*"The future isn't just AI that answers questions. It's AI that takes actions. Agents will book your flights, negotiate deals, and write code, all while you sleep."* ***Sam Altman***

## Building tools, systems, and autonomy

The next frontier of artificial intelligence is all about creating systems that think, act, and execute independently. AI agents represent this evolution. AI agents are intelligent tools capable of reasoning, learning, and taking purposeful action without constant human oversight. Unlike simple chatbots limited to reactive exchanges, these agents proactively solve problems, navigate digital ecosystems, and deliver results with precision.

## The Autonomous Workforce

A useful analogy, though imperfect, is the comparison to self-driving cars. Just as autonomous vehicles perceive their environment, make decisions, and reach destinations without a human driver, AI agents manage workflows, analyze data, schedule operations, and even debug code.

The shift to autonomous systems is forging a new paradigm for entrepreneurship, where solopreneurs and small teams achieve outcomes once requiring entire departments. By delegating repetitive tasks to AI agents, businesses operate with unprecedented efficiency, redirecting human energy toward creativity and strategy.

## AI Agents in Action

Across industries, autonomous systems are already driving transformation. For example, Amazon's AI agents handle thousands of inquiries per minute, processing refunds, tracking orders, and resolving issues without human intervention. In content & development, agents optimize workflows, and troubleshoot code, serving as on-demand specialists and in e-**Commerce,** AI agents personalize recommendations to inventory management streamlining operations on a scale.

AI agents are also available for individual use. Platforms such as Zapier, ChatGPT, and AgentGPT enable users to develop and train custom assistants tailored to their specific workflows.

## Implementing AI Agent

1. **Audit Your Workflow:** Identify repetitive, time-intensive tasks ripe for automation (e.g., email sorting, data aggregation, scheduling).
2. **Start Small, Scale Strategically:** Use no-code tools (Flowise, AgentGPT) to prototype single-task agents before expanding their scope.

3. **Focus on High-Impact Outcomes:** Prioritize automation that frees bandwidth for revenue-generating or creative work.

## The Future of Autonomy

The businesses that thrive will be those leveraging autonomy to remove friction, reduce costs, and reallocate talent toward innovation. The question is not if You will adopt these tools, but how soon You will harness their full potential.

## 10: Creativity And Arts in the AI Age

*"In the Fourth Industrial Revolution, talent, not capital, will be the critical factor of production, geography will matter less than agility.* ***Klaus Schwab***

Creativity defines what it means to be human. It is how we imagine, express, and build what does not yet exist. It is the foundation behind every invention, movement, and masterpiece. We find it not only in art but in how we solve prob- lems, tell stories, and connect with one another. Creativity is how we evolve. Art often begins as pure energy, fully formed in imagination before it takes shape in the physical world. This living expression cannot be coded, replicated, or man- ufactured. It can only be experienced and shared. This is why the rise of AI has influenced artists and creatives.

It challenges our long-held ideas about originality, authorship, and the creative process itself. When machines can generate music, writing, or images in seconds, what does it mean to create something truly unique? And what role does human input play when a single prompt can produce something that looks complete?

These questions deserve serious consideration. Yet the answer may lie in reimagining AI not as a competitor but as a collaborative partner. Intelligent tools can accelerate technical processes, broaden creative possibilities, and spark unexpected inspiration. The essence of artistic work has never been measured by production speed, but by the courage to express depth of feeling and vision. AI can help amplify that expression with greater clarity and impact.

As mentioned earlier in this book, AI is a mimic that operates through pattern recognition. It learns from humanity's collective data, stories, and expressions across time. While it can remix existing ideas, AI cannot experience the present moment's spark of inspiration. It cannot draw from silence or connect to the ineffable sources of creativity. These limitations reveal our enduring advantage as human creators.

Artists and creators can use AI to explore new styles, try fresh compositions, or experiment with color combinations they might not have thought of. Because AI has been trained in so many forms of human expression, it can act as a creative bridge. It allows an artist in one part of the world to draw influence from others across the globe.

In this way, AI becomes a tool for connection and expansion. It helps artists blend, evolve, and grow their work with inspiration drawn from many cultures, styles, and perspectives.

## Creative Integrity and Cultural Respect

Artists, creators, and innovators have always drawn inspiration from cultures, symbols, and traditions around the world. With AI, it is easier than ever to access, remix, and repackage these ideas. But with that ease comes responsibility. Cultural appreciation can be a powerful bridge to understanding, but without context or acknowledgment, it can quickly slip into appropriation, especially when driven by profit rather than respect.

This call for creative integrity is part of a much larger conversation about ethics in the AI era. As the line between human and machine-made blurs, our questions must go beyond aesthetics and into accountability. When AI tools can effortlessly replicate Navajo jewelry designs, Maori facial tattoos, or Balinese dance movements, we must confront essential questions like, are we amplifying or appropriating? Are we compensating or extracting? Are we preserving context or erasing meaning?

Creative integrity means honoring the origins of what moves you. It asks us to slow down, to learn the roots, the stories, and the sacred meaning behind the inspiration we draw from. History offers cautionary tales. Consider Picasso's Cubist revolution, fundamentally shaped by African artifacts he encountered in Parisian museums yet rarely credited. This pattern repeats today when algorithms remix cultural signatures without honoring their origins, turning sacred symbols into disposable aesthetics or spiritual practices into marketing gimmicks. Don't be Picasso.

### How Artists and Creators Can Maintain Authority Over AI

Can an artist lose their creative power to AI? Yes, and it usually happens through overdependence. Like a muscle, creativity weakens without regular exercise. The painter who stops manually mixing colors may lose tactile wisdom. A writer who relies solely on AI may not experience the downloads that can arise from the creative process.

### AI Co-Creation Principles for Artists

**Maintain Creative Friction:** Intentionally preserve the parts of your process that challenge you. Sketch thumbnails by hand. Write first drafts without digital tools. This friction generates artistic fingerprints or unique textures and imperfections no algorithm can replicate. When you outsource to AI too much too soon, you risk diluting what makes your work distinctly yours. The struggle itself shapes your creative identity. Let the resistance guide you, not just the shortcuts.

**Establish AI Guardrails:** Use AI for expansion, never for foundation. Apply the 30/70 Rule: AI handles no more than 30% of creative decision-making and 70% remains as the core vision, original ideas, and creative decisions. This boundary ensures your work remains distinctly human at its heart while leveraging technology for amplification.

**Cultivate Diagnostic Awareness:** Regularly audit your work. "Does this piece still carry my distinctive signature?" "Could another artist using the same prompts produce this?" "What percentage of creative choices originated from me?"

**Protect Skill Development:** Deliberately practice non-AI versions of your work. Traditional painters should maintain life drawing sessions. Writers should keep handwritten journals and Designers should create analog mood boards.

### How Artists and Creators Can Prosper With AI

Prosperity for artists, musicians, writers, and creatives is not about mass production or soulless output. It is about resonance. It is about aligned, liberated, and expansive expression. AI tools can help artists build systems around their cre- ativity, automate marketing, streamline sales, and repurpose content so they have more time and energy to create what's real and meaningful.

For example, a visual artist might use AI to write compelling product descriptions with tools like Copy.ai, schedule posts and content drops with Buffer or Later, and even set up a chatbot to answer common questions from collectors.

Platforms like Zapier act as digital assistants behind the scenes, helping artists build smart, self-sustaining systems. With the right setup, you can automatically post across platforms the moment you upload a file, update your store, or gain a new subscriber.

A musician might use AI to write promotional cop- ies for new releases, generate content ideas tailored to their audience, or build a smart content calendar that keeps fans engaged. AI can also analyze listener data, showing which songs are resonating most with fans.

The same is true for authors and thought leaders. Writing a book is a creative act, but launching it requires strategy, visibility, and consistency. AI can support authors with everything from outlining chapters and creating drafts, using tools like ChatGPT or Claude, to brainstorming podcast pitches and email campaigns with Jasper or Copy.ai.

You can create book trailers and social media con- tent with platforms like Runway, Synthesia, or Pika, and de- sign branded press kits with Canva's AI features. Launch timelines and planning can even be streamlined using AI project assistants like Notion AI or ClickUp AI.

The real power of AI lies in how it supports your vision without replacing it. When used intentionally, it creates space for more clarity, connection, and creative freedom. And prosperity is not just about money, it is also about having the time, presence, and alignment to do more of what matters. With the right systems in place, creators can experience a new kind of abundance. One where they feel supported, seen, and free to focus on what's truly meaningful.

# 11: The Future of AI

*"The real question is, when will we draft an artificial intelligence bill of rights? What will that consist of? And who will get to decide that?"* – ***Gray Scott***

The trajectory of artificial intelligence will be determined not just by technological advancement, but by human awareness, intention, and values. As we have explored throughout this book, AI doesn't exist in a vacuum, it amplifies and reflects the minds that create and use it.

## You Are Human AI

Before we examine machine intelligence, we must first recognize the extraordinary system we already possess: the human mind. Like AI, our brains process information, recognize patterns, and automate responses, shaped by our environment, which can also be considered a form of data.

But thanks to consciousness, we hold an advantage no algorithm can replicate. We have the power to rewire limiting beliefs, our own inner algorithms, choose how we respond to life, and create from imagination rather than just programmed input.

This distinction matters profoundly because, as AI evolves toward Artificial General Intelligence (AGI), the systems we build using our mental output will inevitably inherit our values. In essence, we shape what AI becomes through the energy, beliefs, and intentions we bring to its evolution.

Engaging with AI requires deliberate and informed participation, ensuring that our collective awareness guides its development. The following are five key principles to keep in mind when interacting with AI.

1. **Awareness Over Automation:** Recognize the mental scripts such as cultural, educational, emotional, that you bring with you to AI interactions. conscious users create conscious technology.

2. **Reprogram Your Inner Dataset:** The quality of AI's output depends on human input. Elevate your thinking to elevate what AI produces.

3. **Master Discernment:** In an age of infinite AI-generated content, the ability to distinguish truth from noise becomes a premium skill.

4. **Lead With Values: AI** has no inherent ethics. It adopts ours. Intentionally choose the principles that guide your use of technology.

5. **Imagine Boldly:** Your visions become blueprints for AI's evolution. Think beyond efficiency to consider what world you want to co-create.

## The Ethical Concerns and Challenges of AI

With great power comes great responsibility. As AI systems grow more capable, we must ensure their development and deployment remain fair, transparent, and aligned with human well-being. Addressing AI's ethical challenges requires examining the frameworks that govern it, including questions of access, protection, accountability, and prioritized value.

**Here are some ethical challenges that we could address:**

**Environmental Impact:** Training and running AI models requires massive energy and water mostly drawn from the Earth. Data centers use electricity around the clock, often powered by fossil fuels, and rely on large amounts of water for cooling. If we're not mindful, the tools designed to make life easier could drain the earth's resources. As we build with AI, we must also think about sustainability and choose paths that support both human and environmental well-being.

**Accountability and Ownership:** As AI grows, it is important to remember that humans train it through intention. The data and interactions we provide shape the content AI produces. This raises crucial questions about ownership and fairness. Who truly owns the output created by AI trained on vast amounts of human-generated data? Should companies profit from AI tools built on publicly available information without crediting or compensating those whose work was used? These concerns become even more urgent as AI misclassifies or misidentifies individuals, highlighting the critical need for ethical accountability.

The questions of responsibility must also be answered. When AI systems cause harm, such as a self-driving car crash or an algorithm denying a loan, who should be held accountable? Is it the engineer who designed the system, the company that deployed it, or the user who interacted with it? The answer is not always clear-cut and as AI becomes more integrated into daily life these questions demand serious consideration.

**The Digital Divide and Access Gap:** One of the major ethical concerns is the growing gap between those who have access to the tools, infrastructure, and education to use AI and those who do not. In many parts of the world, reliable internet, modern devices, or even basic digital literacy are still out of reach. This creates an uneven playing field where some communities are left behind while others surge ahead. Access to AI is not just about having the latest technology. It also means having the knowledge, support, and opportunities to use it in ways that create income, solve problems, or improve lives. Without intentional efforts to bridge this gap, AI could deepen existing inequalities rather than solve them.

**Bias in AI:** AI is trained on human data and human data carries bias. We have already seen the consequences: facial recognition tools that misidentify people of color, hiring algorithms that favor certain demographics, and language models that reinforce stereotypes. Developers must work with diverse datasets, create transparent algorithms, and build systems that audit for fairness. Fortunately, programmers have begun creating alternative AI systems that address some of these missing pieces.

**Privacy and Surveillance:** AI thrives on data, and lots of it. Data is the new oil. But this hunger for information raises critical concerns about surveillance, consent, and personal privacy. Governments and corporations now have access to massive amounts of user behavior, preferences, and even emotional patterns. For example, facial recognition systems trained on public data have already been used to track protesters without their consent, raising serious questions about civil liberties and misuse. Regulations like GDPR are a start, but they're not enough. We must push for stronger, global data protection and as individuals, we must stay informed about how our information is collected, stored, and used.

### Keeping up with an AI-Driven Future

**Be a Lifelong Learner:** With AI evolving quickly and knowledge widely available, staying current requires continuous learning. You don't need to code, but understanding AI is beneficial. Take courses, join communities, and stay curious.

**Develop Your Human Strengths:** AI can create content, but it can't match emotional intelligence, empathy, creativity, or spiritual insight. These qualities make your work unique and increasingly valuable as technology advances.

**Integrate AI Rather Than Resist:** Rather than viewing artificial intelligence as a challenge, consider how it may enhance your work. AI can automate routine tasks, allowing you to dedicate more time to creative and strategic initiatives. Additionally, it offers opportunities to broaden your impact and tailor your services. The objective is not to compete with AI, but to collaborate with it so you can concentrate on the uniquely human contributions you provide.

## 12: Some AI Tools to Support Your Journey

*"Copilot isn't just a tool. It's a collaborator. The best AI amplifies human potential, turning friction into flow."* ***Satya Nadella***

### 1. Courses & Digital Products

**Income Range: $500–$50,000/month**

- Entry-Level: Sell $20–50 eBooks or mini-courses, 100 sales = $2–5K.
  Comprehensive $200–500 courses. 50 students = $10–25K.
- Tools: Teachable.

### 2. AI Agents (Automation Services)

**Income Range: $1,000–$20,000/month**

- Basic: $300–500/workflow setup.
  3 clients/week = $4–6K/month.
- $2,000+/month retainer for ongoing automation management.
- Tools: Zapier + Custom GPTs. Most freelancers charge $50–150/hr.

### 3. AI Content Creation

**Income Range: $300–$15,000/month**

- Freelance Writers: \$0.10–0.50/word for AI-assisted content 10K words = \$1–5K.
- Video Creators: \$500–2,000/month selling templated AI videos to small businesses.
- Tools: ChatGPT + Pictory (5x faster output than manual creation)

**4. Personal Brand Monetization**

**Income Range: \$1K–\$100K+/month**

- Newsletters: \$5–50K/month with sponsorships. 5K subscribers = \$2.5–25K.
- Coaching: \$200–5K/client. 10 clients = \$2–50K.
- Tools: ConvertKit (top 10% creators earn 83% of industry revenue).

**5. AI Consulting Services**

**Income Range: \$2K–\$30K/month**

- Prompt Engineering: \$25–150/hour. Avg. \$5K/project
- AI Audits: \$500–3K/report. 2 audits/week = \$4–12K/month.
- Niche Example: AI e-commerce strategists charge 15% of client revenue growth.

### 6. Industry-Specific AI Tools

**Potential Income:**

- Designers: $75–300/hr for AI-assisted graphics using Midjourney and Canva.
- Marketers: 20–50% higher retainers for AI-powered campaigns.
- Educators: 2x course enrollment with AI lesson planners.

### 7. AI Music/Video Production

**Income Range: $500–$25K/month**

- Stock Music: $50–200/track on Soundraw/Boomy . 20 tracks = $1–4K.
- AI Video Services: $100–500/video for businesses using Synthesia and or Runway.

### 8. Global AI Video Tools (2024+)

**Emerging Opportunities:**

- Sora Video Production: Early adopters charge $1.5–3K/min for branded content.
- China Market: Kling AI creators earn $10–50K/month on Douyin.

The income potential examples provided in this guide are based on industry averages, self-reported earnings professionals, and market research. Your actual results will vary based on your Skillset & Experience, time invested, market demand for your specific offerings and economic conditions.

www.ingramcontent.com/pod-product-compliance
Lightning Source LLC
LaVergne TN
LVHW022016200926
848481LV00007B/2427